THREAT POSED BY ELECTROMAGNETIC PULSE (EMP) ATTACK

COMMITTEE ON ARMED SERVICES
HOUSE OF REPRESENTATIVES
ONE HUNDRED TENTH CONGRESS
SECOND SESSION

HEARING HELD
JULY 10, 2008

U.S. GOVERNMENT PRINTING OFFICE

45–133

WASHINGTON : 2009

HOUSE COMMITTEE ON ARMED SERVICES

ONE HUNDRED TENTH CONGRESS

IKE SKELTON, Missouri, *Chairman*

JOHN SPRATT, South Carolina
SOLOMON P. ORTIZ, Texas
GENE TAYLOR, Mississippi
NEIL ABERCROMBIE, Hawaii
SILVESTRE REYES, Texas
VIC SNYDER, Arkansas
ADAM SMITH, Washington
LORETTA SANCHEZ, California
MIKE McINTYRE, North Carolina
ELLEN O. TAUSCHER, California
ROBERT A. BRADY, Pennsylvania
ROBERT ANDREWS, New Jersey
SUSAN A. DAVIS, California
RICK LARSEN, Washington
JIM COOPER, Tennessee
JIM MARSHALL, Georgia
MADELEINE Z. BORDALLO, Guam
MARK E. UDALL, Colorado
DAN BOREN, Oklahoma
BRAD ELLSWORTH, Indiana
NANCY BOYDA, Kansas
PATRICK J. MURPHY, Pennsylvania
HANK JOHNSON, Georgia
CAROL SHEA-PORTER, New Hampshire
JOE COURTNEY, Connecticut
DAVID LOEBSACK, Iowa
KIRSTEN E. GILLIBRAND, New York
JOE SESTAK, Pennsylvania
GABRIELLE GIFFORDS, Arizona
NIKI TSONGAS, Massachusetts
ELIJAH E. CUMMINGS, Maryland
KENDRICK B. MEEK, Florida
KATHY CASTOR, Florida

DUNCAN HUNTER, California
JIM SAXTON, New Jersey
JOHN M. McHUGH, New York
TERRY EVERETT, Alabama
ROSCOE G. BARTLETT, Maryland
HOWARD P. "BUCK" McKEON, California
MAC THORNBERRY, Texas
WALTER B. JONES, North Carolina
ROBIN HAYES, North Carolina
W. TODD AKIN, Missouri
J. RANDY FORBES, Virginia
JEFF MILLER, Florida
JOE WILSON, South Carolina
FRANK A. LoBIONDO, New Jersey
TOM COLE, Oklahoma
ROB BISHOP, Utah
MICHAEL TURNER, Ohio
JOHN KLINE, Minnesota
PHIL GINGREY, Georgia
MIKE ROGERS, Alabama
TRENT FRANKS, Arizona
BILL SHUSTER, Pennsylvania
THELMA DRAKE, Virginia
CATHY McMORRIS RODGERS, Washington
K. MICHAEL CONAWAY, Texas
GEOFF DAVIS, Kentucky
DOUG LAMBORN, Colorado
ROB WITTMAN, Virginia

ERIN C. CONATON, *Staff Director*
RUDY BARNES, *Professional Staff Member*
KARI BINGEN, *Professional Staff Member*
CATERINA DUTTO, *Staff Assistant*

CONTENTS

CHRONOLOGICAL LIST OF HEARINGS

2008

THURSDAY, JULY 10, 2008

THREAT POSED BY ELECTROMAGNETIC PULSE (EMP) ATTACK

STATEMENTS PRESENTED BY MEMBERS OF CONGRESS

WITNESSES

APPENDIX

THREAT POSED BY ELECTROMAGNETIC PULSE (EMP) ATTACK

HOUSE OF REPRESENTATIVES,
COMMITTEE ON ARMED SERVICES,
Washington, DC, Thursday, July 10, 2008.

The committee met, pursuant to call, at 10:05 a.m., in room 2118, Rayburn House Office Building, Hon. Ike Skelton (chairman of the committee) presiding.

OPENING STATEMENT OF HON. IKE SKELTON, A REPRESENTATIVE FROM MISSOURI, CHAIRMAN, COMMITTEE ON ARMED SERVICES

The CHAIRMAN. Good morning. Our committee meets today to receive testimony on the threat of an electromagnetic pulse, EMP, attack.

I want to welcome our distinguished witness, Dr. William Graham—Dr. Graham, if you would assume the witness chair, we would appreciate it—the chairman of this commission that has been assessing this threat.

We look forward to your testimony.

The potential damage that could be caused by an EMP attack on our country is significant, and our committee has long treated this matter seriously. It was this committee that pushed for the authorization of the Commission to Assess the Threat to the United States from EMP Attack as part of the National Defense Authorization Act for 2001. And the committee was pivotal in the re-establishment of the commission in the National Defense Authorization Act for Fiscal Year 2006.

My colleague, Mr. Bartlett, ranking member of the Seapower and Expeditionary Forces Subcommittee, deserves special credit for his dogged and determined attention to this issue.

Our committee held a hearing on this issue in July of 2004, following the release of the commission's executive report, with the commission expected to submit a final report on November the 30th of this year. We thought it was timely to go ahead and have a hearing at this time.

I want the record to note that we invited the Department of Defense (DOD) to testify today. That offer was declined. The Department indicated that an assessment of the EMP threat will be provided to the commission by the Department of Defense later this month. And the Department of Defense prefers to discuss the threat following the release of that threat assessment. I am disappointed we couldn't have them here today, but I understand their reservations. Our committee will work to arrange a forum for the Department of Defense to present its views.

With that, I am certainly interested to hear your testimony, Dr. Graham.

And before we begin, Mr. Hunter, ranking member of California.

STATEMENT OF HON. DUNCAN HUNTER, A REPRESENTATIVE FROM CALIFORNIA, RANKING MEMBER, COMMITTEE ON ARMED SERVICES

Mr. HUNTER. Thank you, Mr. Chairman. And thanks for having this hearing.

And I want to commend, also, Roscoe Bartlett for being the father of EMP on this committee and focusing us on this committee. And I think the statement that the committee heard from the EMP Commission some four years ago in its first report was descriptive of the difficulty and the challenge that EMP poses. And the report concluded that, and I quote, "EMP is one of a small number of threats that can hold our society at risk of catastrophic consequences"—obviously, the ability to impose a great deal of paralysis, both in the economic and security sectors.

So, Mr. Chairman, like you, I am very interested in hearing from the panel. And I want to congratulate Roscoe Bartlett for his enormous dedication to this very important issue. And I look forward to the panel's testimony and our questions after.

Thank you, Mr. Chairman.

The CHAIRMAN. Thank you, Mr. Hunter.

We will proceed, Dr. Graham. And we, again, appreciate your hard work on this commission, and we look forward to your testimony today.

It has been suggested—Dr. Graham, excuse me just a minute—that, as Duncan mentioned, the father of this commission and this issue have a word.

Roscoe Bartlett.

Mr. BARTLETT. Oh, thank you very much. I will take just a moment, because I have a series of questions which I hope will put on the record the real threat that we face here.

Electromagnetic pulse is kind of a spooky kind of thing. And, obviously, there is not very much interest in it, that the seats are largely vacant here, and there are a number of seats down there vacant. The level of interest does not reflect, in any way, the seriousness of this threat, and I hope that that will be apparent by the time this hearing is over.

Thank you.

The CHAIRMAN. With that, Dr. Graham, please proceed.

STATEMENT OF DR. WILLIAM R. GRAHAM, CHAIR, COMMISSION TO ASSESS THE THREAT TO THE UNITED STATES FROM ELECTROMAGNETIC PULSE (EMP) ATTACK

Dr. GRAHAM. Mr. Chairman, members of the committee, thank you for the opportunity to testify today on behalf of the Commission to Assess the Threat to the United States from Electromagnetic Pulse Attack, a commission established through the initiative of this committee and strongly supported by your members.

In accord with the commission's mandate, we are nine members, seven of whom were appointed by the Secretary of Defense and two of whom were appointed by the director of the Federal Emergency

Management Agency. In selecting individuals for appointment to the commission, the appointing officials were directed to consult with the chairman and ranking minority members of the Committees on Armed Services of the Senate and the House of Representatives. So we have your personal scrutiny, as well.

Let me introduce the other members of the commission, who are here today.

The CHAIRMAN. Can you get a little bit closer to the microphone, please?

Dr. GRAHAM. Sure.

The CHAIRMAN. That would help.

Dr. GRAHAM. There.

The CHAIRMAN. Thanks, Doctor.

Dr. GRAHAM. Let me introduce the other members of the commission who are here today.

On my left, starting with General Richard Lawson, a four-star general, retired, from the United States Air Force.

Next to him is Dr. Gordon Soper, a former member of the Defense Nuclear Agency and other nuclear-related functions in the government.

After him is Dr. John Foster, former director of the Livermore National Laboratory and former director of defense research and engineering in the Pentagon, among other distinguished jobs he has held.

And next to him is Dr. Robert Hermann, a former director of the National Reconnaissance Office and long-time associate of the intelligence community.

With your permission, I would like to summarize my prepared statement and submit the full written statement for the record.

An executive report produced by the EMP Commission and delivered to Congress in 2004 provided an overview of the EMP threat to the U.S., our friends and allies, and our deployed forces. Part of the purpose of my testimony today is to introduce a new report produced by the EMP Commission.

This report presents the results of the commission's assessment of an EMP attack to our critical national infrastructures, sometimes referred to as "civilian infrastructures," but since they are as important to our military capabilities and our national security as they are to our civilian economy and citizenship, we chose to call it "critical national infrastructures."

And our report provides recommendations for preparations, monitoring, protection and recovery from such an EMP attack. The assessment is informed by analytic and test activities executed under the commission's sponsorship, which are discussed in the report.

[The information referred to is retained in the committee files and can be viewed upon request.]

Dr. GRAHAM. Several potential adversaries have, and more can, acquire the capability to attack the United States with a high-altitude, nuclear-weapon-generated electromagnetic pulse. A determined adversary can achieve an EMP attack capability without having a high level of sophistication.

EMP is one of a small number of threats that can hold our society at risk of catastrophic consequences. A well-coordinated and widespread cyber attack is another potential example.

EMP will cover a wide geographic region within line of sight of a high-altitude nuclear detonation. The EMP has the capability to produce significant damage to our critical infrastructures and, thus, to the very fabric of U.S. society, as well the ability of the United States, our friends and our allies to project and influence, with military power and other means.

The common element that can produce such an impact from EMP is primarily electronics in the infrastructure, so pervasive in all aspects of our society and military. Our vulnerability is increasing daily, as our use and dependence on electronics and automated systems continues to grow. The impact of EMP is asymmetric, in relation to potential adversaries, who are not as dependent on modern electronics as we are. Much of the efficiency of our society is generated through our use of electronics and automated systems, and that is also a potential vulnerability.

The current vulnerability of our critical infrastructures can both invite and reward attack, if not corrected. Correction is feasible and well within the national means and resources to accomplish over the next few years. As detailed in the commission report provided today to the Congress, the Nation's vulnerability to EMP can be reasonably reduced by coordinated and focused efforts between the private and public sectors of our country.

The appropriate response to the EMP threat is a balance of prevention, planning, training, maintaining situational awareness, protection and preparations for recovery, and doing those in coordination with other potential large-scale threats, such as the cyber threat, and even large-scale man-made threats, such as geomagnetic storms.

In so doing, the U.S. will reduce the incentives for adversaries to conduct such an attack on our homeland, our friends and allies, and our forces deployed abroad. The cost of such improved security in the next three to five years is modest by any standard and extremely so, in relation to both the war on terror and the value of the national infrastructures at risk today.

Although EMP was first considered during the Cold War as a means of paralyzing U.S. retaliatory forces and thereby eliminating our strategic deterrent, the risk of an EMP attack today may be even greater, since several potential adversaries seek nuclear weapons, ballistic missiles, and asymmetric ways to overcome U.S. conventional superiority, using one or a small number of nuclear weapons.

A high-altitude electromagnetic pulse results from the detonation of a nuclear warhead at altitudes above about 25 miles over the country or over our forces. The immediate effect of EMP would be the disruption of and damage to the electronic systems and electrical infrastructure. This, in turn, can seriously impact important aspects of our whole national life, including telecommunications, the financial system, government services, the means of getting food, water, medical care, trade and production, as well as electrical power itself.

Given our Armed Forces' reliance on critical national infrastructures, the cascading failures could seriously jeopardize our military's ability to execute its mission in support of national security. Projection of military power from air bases and seaports requires electricity, fuel, food and water. And the coordination of military operations depends on telecommunications and information systems that are so indispensable to society as a whole. Within the U.S., these assets are, in most cases, obtained by the military from our critical national infrastructures and from civilian providers.

Several potential adversaries have the capability to attack the United States with high-altitude, nuclear-weapon-generated EMP, and others appear to be pursuing efforts to obtain that capability. Long-range ballistic missiles and a high level of technical sophistication are not prerequisites.

For example, such an attack could be launched from a freighter off the U.S. coast, using a short- or medium-range ballistic missile to loft a nuclear warhead to a high altitude, and would not require accuracy in the placement of that warhead. Terrorists sponsored by a rogue state could attempt to execute such an attack, potentially without revealing the identity of their sponsors and even themselves.

Iran has practiced launching a mobile ballistic missile from a vessel in the Caspian Sea. Iran has also tested high-altitude explosions of its Shahab-III ballistic missile, a test mode consistent with EMP attack, and described the test as successful. And, just recently, Iran has tested a series of ballistic missiles, including what it described as a new longer-range variant of the Shahab-III.

Iranian military writings explicitly discuss a nuclear EMP attack that would gravely harm the United States. While the commission does not know the intention of Iran in conducting these activities, we are disturbed by the capability that emerges when we connect all of these dots. In fact, I don't have another explanation for the high-altitude detonation of the Shahab-III and some of the Iranian tests or the launch off the Caspian Sea, other than to deploy an EMP type of attack.

Relatively low-yield, unsophisticated nuclear weapons can be employed to generate potentially catastrophic EMP effects over wide geographic areas. And designs for variances of such weapons, as well as more sophisticated weapons, appear to have been illicitly trafficked for a quarter-century at least.

Recently, it has been reported in the press that United Nations investigators found that the design for an advanced nuclear weapon able to fit on ballistic missiles currently in the inventory of Iran, North Korea, and other potentially hostile states was in the possession of Swiss nationals affiliated with the AQ Khan nuclear proliferation network. This suggested nuclear weapons designs may already be in the possession of hostile states that sponsor terrorism. It also suggests that it would be a mistake to judge the status and sophistication of nuclear weapon programs based solely on the indigenous national capabilities, since outside assistance from proliferators is probably the norm.

EMP effects from nuclear bursts are not new threats to our Nation. What is different now is that some potential sources of EMP threats are difficult to deter. They may be may rogue regimes or terrorist groups that have no state identity. They may have only one or a few nuclear weapons and be motivated to attack the U.S. without regard for their own safety.

China and Russia have considered limited nuclear attack option that, unlike their Cold War plans, employ EMP as the primary or sole means of attack. Indeed, in May 1999, during the NATO bombing of the former Yugoslavia, high-ranking members of the Russian Duma, meeting with the U.S. congressional delegation to discuss the Balkans conflict, raised the specter of a Russian EMP attack that would paralyze the United States.

As recently as two weeks ago, Assistant Secretary of Defense for Asian and Pacific Security Affairs James J. Shinn testified before this committee that China's military is working on exotic electromagnetic pulse weapons that can devastate electronic systems by using a burst of energy similar to that produced by a nuclear blast.

Another key difference from the past is that the U.S. has developed, more than most nations, as a modern society heavily dependent on electrical power, electronics, telecommunications, information networks, and an extensive set of financial and transportation systems that leverage modern technology. This asymmetry is a source of substantial economic, industrial, societal, and military advantage for the U.S., but the critical interdependencies and normally reliable operation of the infrastructures creates potential vulnerabilities, if multiple simultaneous disruptions and failures can be made to occur, since they almost never occur under normal operations of these infrastructures.

Therefore, terrorists or state actors that possess one or a few relatively unsophisticated nuclear-armed missiles may well calculate that instead of, or in addition to, destroying a city or a military base, they could obtain the greatest economic-political-military utility from conducting an EMP attack, while experiencing the lowest risk of being intercepted or otherwise stopped before they are able to detonate the weapon.

The commission has offered a series of recommendations intended to reduce the risk and consequences of an EMP attack. These include pursuing intelligence, interdiction, and deterrence, to discourage an EMP attack; protecting critical components of the infrastructure, especially those requiring long periods of time to replace. In particular, the U.S. military needs to determine what elements of the national infrastructure are critical to its continued operations and how to either protect or circumvent failures of that infrastructure.

Next would be maintaining the capability to monitor and evaluate the condition of the critical infrastructures; then, recognizing how an EMP attack differs from other forms of infrastructure disruption and damage, since its effects would not occur under normal operation of our generally reliable infrastructure systems.

Planning to carry out a systematic recovery of critical infrastructures would be very important; and that is a planning function. That is not a hugely expensive undertaking, but it is one that requires thought and effort and time; then, training, evaluating, redteaming, and periodically reporting to you and other Members of Congress of the status of the country in being able to respond to an EMP attack.

Defining the government's responsibility to act, because, surely, the defense of the country is a shared responsibility between the government and the private sector; but defending the country is primarily a government responsibility, and providing a normally reliable infrastructure is largely a private sector responsibility.

Recognizing the opportunity for shared benefits in dealing with other forms of widespread attack, such as I had mentioned, cyber attack or naturally occurring events. Probably something about the size of Katrina would be the smallest size that we are considering here.

And, finally, conducting research to better understand the infrastructure systems' vulnerability to EMP and other threats and developing cost-effective solutions for mitigating them.

Finally, allow me to give you a preview of the EMP Commission's findings, to date, for its next report, which you have directed us to provide and due to the Congress in November, which will assess the progress being made to protect the Nation and, particularly, our military capabilities from EMP attack. The commission is receiving cooperation from a number of federal agencies and working closely with them to derive that information.

While measures to establish a balance of prevention, planning, training, situational awareness, protection, and preparations will require a sustained effort, the commission wishes to note an increased focus within the Defense Department since it received the commission's earlier reports and with your continued interest. Our report to the Congress, due in November, will address this in more detail, as part of our required assessment of the DOD's progress in implementing the steps necessary to mitigate the attack.

The United States faces a long-term challenge to maintain technical competence for understanding and managing the effects of nuclear weapons, including EMP. The Department of Energy and the National Nuclear Security Administration have developed and implemented an extensive nuclear weapons stockpile stewardship program over the last decade. However, no such comparable effort was initiated to understand the effects that nuclear weapons produce on modern systems.

The commission reviewed current national capabilities to understand and to manage the effects of EMP and concluded that the Federal Government does not today have sufficient human and physical resources and assets for reliably assessing and managing EMP threats. And the U.S. is rapidly losing the remaining technical competence and facilities that it needs in government, in the national laboratories, and in the industrial community.

EMP attack on the critical infrastructures is a serious problem, but one that can be managed at reasonable cost. A serious national commitment to address the threat of an EMP attack can lead to an integrated national posture that would significantly reduce the payoff for such an attack and allow the United States to recover from EMP and from other threats, man-made and natural, to the critical national infrastructures.

A failure to do so will not only leave the critical national infrastructures that are necessary for our society to function at risk, but will also place our ability to conduct military operations in severe jeopardy.

This concludes my prepared statement, Mr. Chairman. Thank you again. And I look forward to an opportunity for myself and my colleagues and fellow commissioners to respond to your questions.

[The prepared statement of Dr. Graham can be found in the Appendix on page 35.]

Mr. SPRATT [presiding]. Dr. Graham, thank you very much indeed.

You have a distinguished panel of colleagues sitting behind you, and I will take the liberty of presiding at this point and invite any one of them who would like to add to your comments to take this opportunity to do so.

Dr. Foster.

Mr. FOSTER. No, thank you, sir.

Mr. SPRATT. I didn't want to get this distinguished panel here and not at least give you the opportunity to say something further, if you wish.

Dr. GRAHAM. Mr. Henry Kluepfel has joined us, too, as another commissioner sitting there. I didn't introduce him initially, but I would like do that now. Extensive background in telecommunications.

Mr. SPRATT. I want to turn now to Mr. Bartlett, because he is the person who requested this hearing and the reason that we are meeting here today.

And, Roscoe, the floor is yours to ask questions as you see fit.

Mr. BARTLETT. Thank you very much.

I was sitting in that hotel room in Vienna, Austria, with a number of other Members of Congress and three members of the Russian government—Vladimir Lukin, who was the ambassador here at the end of Bush I and the beginning of the Clinton Administration; Alexander Shabanov, who I think was the third-ranking communist; and Vladimir Rushkov, a young, aspiring Russian.

Vladimir Lukin was very angry, and he sat with his arms folded, looking at the ceiling, for a couple of days during these discussions. We developed a framework agreement, which, about a half a dozen days later, was adopted by the G–8 and ended the Kosovo controversy.

At one point, Vladimir Lukin looked up. He said, "If we really wanted to hurt you, with no fear of retaliation, we would launch an SLBM [submarine-launched ballistic missile] from the ocean, detonate a nuclear weapon high above your country, and shut down your power grid and your communications for six months or so." And Alexander Shabanov, the handsome, blond communist, smiled and said, "And if one weapon wouldn't do it, we have some spares, like about 10,000, I think." This kind of puts in context the threat that we face.

I read a prepublication copy of a book called *One Second After*. I hope it does get published; I think the American people need to read it. It was the story of a ballistic missile EMP attack on our country. The weapon was launched from a ship off our shore, and then the ship was sunk so that there were no fingerprints. The weapon was launched about 300 miles high over Nebraska, and it shut down our infrastructure countrywide.

The story runs for a year. It is set in the hills of North Carolina. At the end of the year, 90 percent of our population is dead; there are 25,000 people only still alive in New York City. The communities in the hills of North Carolina are more lucky: only 80 percent of their population is dead at the end of a year.

I understand that this is a realistic assessment of what a really robust EMP laydown could do to our country?

Dr. GRAHAM. We think that is in the correct range. We don't have experience with losing the infrastructure in a country with 300 million people, most of whom don't live in a way that provides for their own food and other needs. We can go back to an era when people did live like that. That would be—10 percent would be 30 million people, and that is probably the range where we could survive as a basically rural economy.

Mr. BARTLETT. It is my understanding that, in interviewing some Russian generals, that they told you that the Soviets had developed a "super-EMP" enhanced weapon that could produce 200 kilovolts per meter at the center?

Dr. GRAHAM. Yes, Mr. Bartlett. We engaged two senior Russian generals—who were also lecturers and authors from their general staff academy, who had written about advanced weapons—and actually brought them over to the U.S. and spent a day meeting with them and questioning them about EMP-type weapons; and they said a number of interesting things. One was that, in fact, the Russians had developed what they called the "super-EMP" weapon that could generate fields in the range of 200 kilovolts per meter. And we had seen in other open literature that the Russians appeared to be using that figure as an upper bound for the kind of EMP that could be produced by nuclear weapons. So, we weren't surprised, too surprised, to see it.

They also told us that both there were Russian and other technologists, engineers and scientists, who were working with North Korea and receiving Western wages, they emphasized, helping North Korea with the design of its nuclear weapons.

So, we found it extremely interesting in talking to them.

Mr. BARTLETT. This is about, what, four times higher than anything that we ever built or tested to, in terms of EMP hardening?

Dr. GRAHAM. Yes.

Mr. BARTLETT. Which means that, even if you were some hundreds of miles away from that, that it would be somewhere in the range of 50 to 100 kilovolts per meter at the margins of our country, for instance?

Dr. GRAHAM. Yes. Over much of the margin, yes.

Mr. BARTLETT. So, we aren't sure that much of our military would still be operable after that robust laydown. Is that correct?

Dr. GRAHAM. We just don't have test data to tell us one way or the other.

Mr. BARTLETT. I also understand that we aren't certain that we could launch, through a series of robust EMP laydowns, that we could launch our intercontinental ballistic missiles.

Dr. GRAHAM. We designed both the missiles and their bases and the strategic communication systems during the Cold War to be able to survive and operate through EMP fields on the order of 50 kilovolts per meter, which was our concern at the time, before we realized that weapons could be designed that had larger EMP fields.

We added margin to the protection of those systems. And to the extent that they have maintained that hardness, they would survive greater than 50 kilovolts per meter, but I don't think we have any data telling us how much greater.

Mr. BARTLETT. I would just like to spend a moment looking at the national infrastructure of our country. It is my understanding that a robust laydown, likely to be produced by a single weapon of 200 kilovolts per meter that made it 300 miles high over Iowa or Nebraska, would probably shut down all of our national infrastructure. There would be no electricity. That Supervisory Control and Data Acquisition (SCADA) units in our sub-stations and so forth would all be gone. The large transformers would be destroyed. And we don't make those; it would take a year and a half or so to buy them from somebody overseas who makes them.

We would then be in a world, it is my understanding, where the only person you could talk to is the person next to you, unless you happen to be a ham operator with a vacuum tube set, which is a million times less susceptible. And the only way you could go anywhere is to walk, unless you happened to have a car that had coil-end distributor and you could get some gasoline to put in it.

Is that a pretty accurate description of the world we would be in?

Dr. GRAHAM. We did conduct tests of SCADAs, automobiles, and other systems. And while, as a commission, we don't have either the funds or the staff that would be needed to do a comprehensive test of those, all of the data we did obtain indicate that your description is accurate.

Mr. BARTLETT. Your initial report came out about four years ago. We have had four years in which we could have been doing something to protect—I am very concerned that we don't have the equivalent of an insurance policy. It is unlikely my home will burn, but I would not sleep well tonight if it did not have an insurance policy. I don't hire somebody to stand there watching for a fire, to yell, "Fire, fire," but I do have an insurance policy. That is what I would like my Nation to have for an EMP protection.

We don't have anything near that, do we?

Dr. GRAHAM. No, we don't.

The commission has been trying for over a year, through working with the Department of Homeland Security and the Homeland Security Council staff in the White House, to look at the 15 canonical scenarios they have defined as potential terrorist threats to the U.S., which included a nuclear weapon; but it is a nuclear weapon going off at ground level in a city, to either add to that as another category of nuclear weapon attack or add a 16th scenario of a high-altitude EMP attack. But as yet, we have been unable to obtain their cooperation in adding that threat to the homeland security threat list.

Mr. BARTLETT. I would just like to end by re-emphasizing what you emphasized in your testimony. A terrorist group, not even a nation group, but a terrorist group with a tramp steamer and a Scud launcher and a crude nuclear weapon, and if they miss by 100 miles, it doesn't matter, does it?

Dr. GRAHAM. No.

Mr. BARTLETT. And they could launch that weapon and shut down, what, all of New England?

Dr. GRAHAM. Yes, probably with a Scud-B they could cover essentially all of the East Coast or all of the West Coast. And the coasts tend to be where most of the population is.

Mr. BARTLETT. Which would be Katrina how many times over?

Dr. GRAHAM. Oh, several times over.

Mr. BARTLETT. At least an order of magnitude.

Dr. GRAHAM. Something on that size, yes.

Mr. BARTLETT. The average city has a three-day supply of food?

Dr. GRAHAM. I think that is about what we estimated.

Mr. BARTLETT. Okay.

Well, I want to thank you very much.

I am very appreciative, Mr. Chairman, that you set up this hearing.

I think that, as the testimony indicated, I think this is the most asymmetric attack that could occur in our country. Am I wrong in that? Can you think of any more asymmetric attack on our country?

Dr. GRAHAM. I think there are very few that go with this. One, as I mentioned, was a cyber attack, possibly a very widespread and contagious biological attack. But this is one of a very small set and very asymmetric.

Mr. BARTLETT. Doesn't our very vulnerability invite this kind of an attack?

Dr. GRAHAM. Yes, Mr. Bartlett. That is our primary concern, that if the country does nothing about it, we are essentially advertising to a world which already has a good understanding of the implications of EMP and has written about it extensively. Not just from the U.S., but in our survey of potentially hostile countries, they talk about this extensively in the open literature, and did before the commission was even established. And it is a very asymmetric situation that we could face.

Mr. BARTLETT. I have been told that I shouldn't be talking about this because it gives our adversaries ideas. They already know about this, correct?

Dr. GRAHAM. They knew about it before the commission was ever established. And that was the first thing we checked. We said, "How much can we say without giving away information that isn't available to our adversaries"? And when we reviewed the literature, why, we found there was an extensive knowledge of EMP and its effects widespread.

Mr. BARTLETT. Why is there so little interest on the part of our leadership to do something about this? Is it just too hard? They just don't want to face it?

Dr. GRAHAM. That is a good question. It might be better to ask a sociologist than an engineer and physicist that question.

But it falls into the category of a problem which hasn't happened yet. Certainly, our ability to predict very unusual and significant events, whether it is Pearl Harbor, the start of the Korean War, 9/11 and whatever—we have, to paraphrase Winston Churchill, much to be humble about in our ability to predict these events before they happen. Of course, once they happen, then there tends to be a massive response. But somehow it is just not within our character and our society to look for these events before they occur.

Mr. BARTLETT. Thank you very much, Mr. Chairman, for setting up this hearing—and I look forward to the additional questions and responses. Thank you.

The CHAIRMAN [presiding]. Mr. Solomon Ortiz, please.

Mr. ORTIZ. Thank you so much for your testimony.

This is really—it is scary. Sometimes we think that this is something that might never happen, but I agree with what my good friend, Mr. Roscoe Bartlett, asked. We would feel a lot better if we had some type of insurance or some type of shield that would protect us from dismantling all the equipment that we have.

But based on increasing dependence on advanced electronic systems, have you, has the Department of Defense and Department of Homeland Security adequately addressed or implemented any of the EMP Commission's, the previous recommendations to protect the United States from attack?

Dr. GRAHAM. Mr. Ortiz, the Department of Defense has begun a process to address that.

About two years ago, in response to the mandate of the first legislation establishing the commission, the Secretary of Defense issued a directive to the Department with a series of actions he wanted to see carried out to address EMP. And the Department of Defense has started working down that list.

I would characterize them today as in the planning stage, trying to identify what their requirements are, what the issues they have to address are, and trying to set up some kind of an organizational structure to address them.

So, the DOD is early in the process, and I would say that the other parts of the government have not yet begun any process.

Mr. ORTIZ. And I know we are looking at what might happen to us if they detonate a missile over the United States. But on the other side, what can we do to defend ourselves? From what I hear, I don't think we have anything to defend ourselves. Am I correct when I say that?

Dr. GRAHAM. No, I think there are several things we can do.

Mr. ORTIZ. That is what I would like to hear.

Dr. GRAHAM. I think the first thing is to recognize the problem and let other countries know that we understand what might happen and we are taking steps to mitigate that.

Another step early on would be to identify those parts of the infrastructure that are most likely to be damaged and, particularly, the ones that are hardest to replace and focus on those, to protect them.

Let me give you an example of that. August 13, 2003, a power transmission line got hot enough that it sagged down and touched a tree and shorted the ground, and that dropped that power transmission line. And for the next hour, 2,000 megawatts of generating capacity kept looking for a route to get to the north-central part of the United States. And as that power switched from one transmission system to another, it kept overloading them and dropping them, as well, until finally the whole Northeast, with very few exceptions, was blacked out. Because the protection circuitry in the power system was properly arranged, nothing was damaged in our power system during that outage, and within the next two days, the country was able to bring back the power to that area.

The problem with EMP is that protection circuitry itself and the protection systems, many of which are based on these SCADA computers, would be damaged. They would be damaged immediately, and therefore they could not provide proper protection immediately and could lead to the damage of other parts of the system, including things such as large power transformers and switches.

So, building these small, relatively inexpensive control devices, SCADAs, which are changed out every few years, anyway, in a way so they won't fail from EMP, and, particularly, won't be damaged by EMP, is, in our view, an important step and one that we would like to encourage the government and the private sector to work together on. And, in fact, the commission has a plan to build a demonstration model of a protected SCADA, so that we can show people it is not either terribly expensive or terribly difficult to do that.

But recognizing what has happened, since this would be very unusual, is a key to our response. It is quite possible that the system operators will do more damage to the system after an EMP event in trying to recover the system, if they don't know what has happened; and it is not expensive to recognize this, but we don't have the means to do that today.

So, there are a whole number of steps that we could carry out that would be very effective and not hugely expensive.

Let me ask my colleagues on the commission if any of them have further comments on that.

Okay.

Mr. ORTIZ. My time is up, so thank you so much for your testimony and answering our questions. Thank you, sir.

Dr. GRAHAM. Thank you.

The CHAIRMAN. Mr. McHugh from New York.

Mr. McHUGH. Thank you, Mr. Chairman.

Sixteen years on this committee, as I was chatting with Mr. Bartlett before—we have been honored by many distinguished panelists, and I am being totally serious when I say rarely have we been so honored as we are here, this morning, to have gathered such a body of distinguished individuals with such a great record of service.

And thank you for taking up such an important issue that no one seems to be concerned about. And we certainly are in debt to Mr. Bartlett, as others have mentioned, for his leadership on this, but you really have really put a fine point to it.

My friend from Texas, Mr. Ortiz, said it is scary. As you read through these pages, you talk about people stuck for long periods on elevators, airplanes crashing, no water, no food. The difference between this and Stephen King is that Stephen King in Borders is in the fiction section; this report is not. And I hope, if nothing else comes of it, this helps to focus our Nation's attention on the unknown.

I was very distressed to hear that one of the reasons, perhaps, the Department of Homeland Security has not yet responded—and I realize it is speculation—but that it is a threat unknown to this point. That is the purpose of the Department of Homeland Security, it seems to me, to contemplate and ultimately to take steps to guard against the unexperienced, the unknown, such as 9/11 was to that point. So, if that is their mindset, I trust they will begin to rethink it very, very quickly.

As I was reading through, on page 156, you use the phrase "graceful degradation." I like the term. Can you tell me a little bit about what it would mean in its application, with respect to protection from EMP?

Dr. GRAHAM. Yes. We don't envision the country having the resources to try to protect everything in the civilian infrastructure. It is a massive infrastructure, and, in fact, elements of it do fail from time to time. But normally, when they fail, it starts at a single-point failure, and the failure is contained, and the system is left in a configuration where the infrastructure can be re-established, such as it was in that August 2003 Northeast blackout or other blackouts we have had.

We think we could properly protect and contain and design the infrastructure protection in such a way that, while the infrastructure might go down for a limited period of time, it wouldn't be so damaged that it couldn't be brought back into functionality within the period of time that people can get along without it.

And that is our view of graceful degradation: failing in such a way that it is not suffering large, permanent damage that can't be replaced within a short period of time, but rather, basically, make it so this can be reset and re-established and brought up in a systematic way.

Mr. McHUGH. I realize the scope of this challenge is, to say the least, multifaceted, and there is no one prescriptive response. But the concept of graceful degradation, as I was reading through, seemed to be both technologically achievable and, in a relative sense, pretty affordable. Am I being overly optimistic, or would that be a fair judgment?

Dr. GRAHAM. Well, affordability is like beauty; it tends to be in the eye of the beholder. But it seems to us that, compared to the cost of the infrastructure or the cost of the failure of the infrastructure from EMP, if it were to occur, the cost of the analysis, then the planning, then the protection of key elements and the testing and exercise and maintaining situational awareness, all of those are very modest costs.

Mr. McHUGH. Just one final question; I just have a few seconds left here. You mentioned you are charged with doing an assessment of DOD's steps in this regard. Do you have a time frame, a calendar on when that will be achieved?

Dr. GRAHAM. Yes. Our legislative mandate specifies that we deliver to you a report by the end of November of this year. And we are well under way working on it now.

Mr. McHUGH. Well, again, gentlemen, thank you so much for your service and to Mr. Bartlett for his insight, and look forward to your continued efforts.

Thank you, Mr. Chairman.

The CHAIRMAN. Thank the gentleman.

The gentleman from South Carolina, Mr. Spratt.

Mr. SPRATT. Dr. Graham, thank you very much and your entire panel for the excellent presentation you have made and for the work you have done.

This is truly the all-time asymmetric threat, but it is also the all-time esoteric threat. It is not widely understood, although it is not beyond the apprehension and the comprehension of our most insidious enemies.

In your work thus far, what can you say about the sufficiency of the level of attention amongst our commanders and leaders at the national level to this particular threat and to what can be done to counter the threat? Is there a sufficient level of national awareness?

Dr. GRAHAM. I would say there are shining points in our national leadership's interest, but only a few.

The Secretary of Defense has directed the Defense Department to carry out an orderly program. General Chilton, in particular, the commander of the Strategic Command, has taken a great deal of interest in this and is working hard on the systems under his command and operation to assure that our strategic forces will be survivable and effective under EMP.

I think it is at the bottom of the list, in many areas, certainly in the Defense Department, but it is also in the Department of Homeland Security, where this has not yet received much attention or much thought.

Mr. SPRATT. You have given us a message first of the bad news, which is a wake-up call, and then the good news, and that is there are remedial steps we can take and, for the most part, they are affordable.

But as you describe the scope and potential of this kind of attack, recognizing that it could affect even the telecommunications network and the electric power grid in this country, the cost, just off the back of an envelope, would seem to be enormous to protect all of these devices.

You can understand how hardening satellites, and in particular future-launch satellites, is within our capability to afford, but the entire electric grid, the entire telecommunications system, all of these things nationwide, aren't we talking about some substantial financial commitment?

Dr. GRAHAM. Well, it would be a large order. There is no doubt of that. The work would have the effect of increasing the reliability of that infrastructure in the first instance, which is a reasonable activity for the providers of the infrastructure and something they could ask to put in their rate basis.

To the extent that we are dealing just with the national security aspects, that is a government function. But we found the cooperation and interest in the cooperation between the private sector and with the government to be very good. For example, we have worked with the North American Energy Reliability Corporation, which tries to increase the reliability of the power grid under a number of different scenarios, and they are certainly willing to cooperate on this with the government. So, if we can arrange for the government to contribute to the national security part and the private sector infrastructure to contribute to the overall reliability part, we think there is a union of effort that can make this happen in a less than extremely costly fashion and do it in such a way that we actually ramp up the effort based on knowledge, rather than try to swamp the problem with funds.

Mr. SPRATT. One last question. From where we sit as Members of Congress, as the Armed Services Committee, what can we best do to extract this kind of commitment and to see that it is followed through in a programmatic way?

Dr. GRAHAM. I think requesting from the Defense Department and the military forces their appraisal of potentially vulnerable systems and a description of efforts they are undertaking to deal with that, along with their programmatic requests for the resources necessary to address and manage that, would be a very effective first step.

I think a continued interest on your part, that you have shown in establishing this commission, has had a large effect, already, on the activities in the Defense Department. And a continued interest either through this commission or some other function will continue to keep the pressure on the Administration to work this problem.

Mr. SPRATT. Thank you again. And thank you to the entire panel for the work you have done. Thank you.

The CHAIRMAN. I thank the gentleman.

Mr. Franks, please.

Mr. FRANKS. Well, thank you, Mr. Chairman.

And thank you, Dr. Graham.

You know, I am reminded, historically, that people such as yourselves have been profoundly important to the success of this country. I know that Dr. Otto Hahn was playing with the atomic bomb scenario in Germany a long time ago. And it turns out that one Albert Einstein kind of beat him to the draw, and he happened to be on our side, and we can all be very grateful for that. So, I appreciate you and all your colleagues. You are the invisible frontline of freedom here, and we are very grateful to you.

I happen to have been here on the committee when you addressed us some two or three years ago and have been very concerned about the EMP situation since then, and appreciate Roscoe Bartlett, or Congressman Bartlett, for his leadership in this area.

I wanted to ask you a question related to our national security space systems. I am sure General Shelton has had many conversations with you about that. Are there things that we can do or should do to protect that vital national security asset against the EMP capability?

Dr. GRAHAM. Yes, Mr. Franks. There are things we can do. In the first instance, we need to assess the status of the ground links of the space systems we have. That is, on the one hand, satellites that are at very high orbits—geosynchronous orbits or even semisynchronous orbits—are high enough that the pumping of the Van Allen Belts by the exoatmospheric nuclear explosions won't cause much degradation for those satellites. Low-altitude satellites that fly into intense parts of Van Allen Belts would probably fail after an exoatmospheric explosion within a few days to a week or two, and, in fact, that happened after the STARFISH test that we conducted in the Pacific in the early 1960's. But all of these satellite systems—geosync, semisync, low-altitude—use ground links to get their information to the users on the surface, and all of those ground facilities would be exposed if they are underneath, within line of sight of a high-altitude nuclear event.

And, of course, then we have to trace back from the ground site itself to where it gets its power, where it provides its telecommunications, what personnel it needs to be operated, and so on. So, an assessment can be made of that, and that can lead to some useful steps taken to provide for those after high-altitude nuclear bursts—an EMP event, for example.

Mr. FRANKS. Well, thank you.

I know you mentioned—I think Dr. Bartlett mentioned some discussions with Duma representatives, and they said, you know, if we had wanted to—the intent here is a very, very important consideration for those who have the EMP capability. And my concern is—and I don't want to get into anything classified here, and you will have to help me to make sure I don't, even though I know that you have said that most people already know so much more about this than we have already been aware of for a long time—but intent is everything. My concern is a nation like Iran, with some of their advanced missile capabilities that are developing more and more all the time—well, what size of a warhead and what heights would be necessary for, say, someone like Iran? Are they approaching that capability in terms of their missile capability? And would a crude warhead—or what kind of, you know, a kiloton warhead is necessary? And discuss the enhanced warhead terminology, so that we can understand what needs—you know, is this regular atomic warheads? Does this have to be something on the size of a W88? Or give us a picture here of what we are really facing and what Iran's potential capability might be against us.

Dr. GRAHAM. Since one of the members of the commission, Dr. Foster, was the director of the Livermore National Laboratory and, as far as I know, still has the most advanced nuclear weapon design that we use for one of the types of—one of the aspects of the nuclear weapon, and that is after probably approaching 30 or more years, I would like to ask him to address the nuclear weapon question. Oh, he left? He had another meeting to go to, unfortunately. Okay. I will try to fill in, but not as well as Dr. Foster.

I will tell you what I have learned from him in this process, that you can—you will get potentially catastrophic EMP from even a first-generation nuclear weapon. It doesn't have to be optimized for this purpose. So, any nuclear weapon that can be obtained and put on a missile, which means that the weight in the one-ton or less range for most of the missiles we have talked about, would produce the EMP effects we described. There are nuclear weapon designs that we know about and that the Russians clearly know about, and possibly others know about, which produce stronger and stronger EMP fields. And in all these cases, the weapon yield itself doesn't have to be more than 10 kilotons or so. It doesn't take a very large nuclear weapon or a very large yield to produce these effects. They are produced by the gamma rays that come out. They come out very quickly, and it is the first part of the nuclear detonation process.

So, any nuclear weapon in the hands of potential adversaries would be bad news for us, in this regard.

Mr. FRANKS. Well, thank you, sir.

And thank you, Mr. Chairman. I am hoping that the committee recognizes that the coincidence of terrorism and technologies, such as we are discussing today, represents a grave threat to the human family.

Mr. SPRATT [presiding]. Mr. Taylor.

Mr. TAYLOR. Thank you, Dr. Graham. A couple of things—and I very much appreciate what your committee is doing—a couple of quick questions, and I know they won't be quick answers.

I am a proponent of a nuclear Navy to protect—particularly more nuclear-powered ships. I would be curious if your commission has looked at our surface fleet and determined whether or not a nuclear-powered ship was any more or less susceptible to an EMP than a conventionally powered ship.

The second thing I would like you to comment on is there have been recent articles that strongly suggest that part of the traumatic brain injuries that are coming out of the conflicts in Iraq and Afghanistan might have been caused by the effects of EMP on the brain, in addition to the shock waves. I was wondering—and I have only read this article this week, and so I don't know if your commission had the time to even look at that and if there has been any talk amongst your commission, since you are the experts, of how we might counter that for the individual soldier.

Last, without talking out of school, I think it is fair to say that several contractors are looking at ways of having a handheld-directed EMP for the purpose of disabling fast boats that are running drugs or, possibly, a vehicle-borne IED that is coming at you. So, if there are contractors out there looking at them for good purposes to protect Americans, it is a pretty safe bet that somewhere in the world, someone is also looking at the same thing, which could, for example, fry the electricity going to Wall Street and, certainly, cause a great deal of disruption, or you can think of any number of scenarios. I was wondering if you could touch on those subjects, then, that I just posed to you.

Dr. GRAHAM. Let me take them in reverse order. As a commission, we focused on the nuclear EMP problem, which is a very wide-area problem. We did note that devices can be made, and don't require huge power supplies to operate, which can produce intense electromagnetic fields over very small regions; but they are regions of the order of tens of feet to maybe hundreds of feet, but not miles and hundreds and thousands of miles, like the EMP. So, for local effects, it is a possible course to pursue, certainly.

As far as the brain injuries goes——

Mr. TAYLOR. Sir, if I may, on a one-by-one basis, are you proposing safeguards against something like that, a handheld-directed EMP going after America's economic infrastructure on Wall Street? Are you proposing safeguards? And if you are, which agency of our Nation should be taking the lead on that?

Dr. GRAHAM. We have not addressed that directly, because, in part, we focused on the high-altitude nuclear problem, and, in part, it seems to us that that was an issue related to physical security, but one which is in addition to the normal threat of truck bombs or bombs or rocket-propelled grenades or things of that sort. While the range of the EMP would be—of the conventionally generated EMP would be comparable to these other threats, the effects and the protection against it would be different.

And so, for example, electromagnetic shielding would be an important aspect of that, but we have not gone down that path in our own studies. We think it is a good issue for high-priority facilities to follow. But we did note that in terms of critical infrastructures, even the best of them fail. The trouble is they fail at single-point failures, and the operators are good at circumventing single-point failures. What they don't practice and don't know how to address is when they have multiple failures over a wide area nearly simultaneously, and that is the problem that the nuclear EMP brings to bear.

Mr. TAYLOR. For traumatic brain injuries, did you look into that?

Dr. GRAHAM. On that, we did not look into that, and I have no information on that, so I am afraid I can't be of any help.

Mr. TAYLOR. Are nuclear-powered surface ships being any more or less protected?

Dr. GRAHAM. I have looked at the hardening and protection of ships at various times over the last several decades, and my impression is that protecting nuclear-powered ships is certainly no more difficult than protecting conventionally powered ships.

Mr. TAYLOR. Thank you, sir.

Thank you, Mr. Chairman.

The CHAIRMAN [presiding]. I thank the gentleman.

Mr. Saxton.

Mr. SAXTON. Thank you.

Dr. Graham, your description of the threat is certainly sobering and, I am sure, accurate. And I am just curious to know whether you have—I am sure you have given thought to what our defenses against an EMP laydown might be from—back to the nuclear device. I would think we would want to look at a robust missile defense system, and I would also think that the midcourse or boost phase would be the place that you would want to be capable, relative to this EMP threat, rather than the phase that we are in now that we can accurately use PATRIOT and the aero-type defenses. Would you comment for us on that?

Dr. GRAHAM. Yes, Mr. Saxton. First, there is no magic bullet to solving the EMP problem, so I believe we need to look at a large number of steps we can take and look for the most cost-effective approach with each of them and try to combine them in a useful manner.

Certainly, one of the things we can do is look to the ballistic missile defense capabilities that we have developed and deployed. For very long-range missiles that might come over the U.S., the ground-based missile defense could have an effective role in intercepting the carrier missile before the bomb goes off and as early as possible. And second, even for shorter-range missiles such as the Scuds or the Shahab–3s or other short-range missiles to medium-range missiles that could be fired off our shores, we have a large fleet of Aegis ships, and several of those have the Standard Missile–3, which is an interceptor missile designed to destroy offensive missiles. And by being able to move those ships around and turn on the radars from time to time and see what is going on offshore, we could at least increase the uncertainty that any potential attacker would have in being able to successfully launch an offshore, ship-based attack.

That system has proven to be extremely reliable and effective. I think the last interceptor did shoot down a satellite, in fact, but it can shoot down things at considerably lower altitudes than that.

So, using our missile defense assets both to deter, dissuade, and, if necessary, intercept missiles going over the U.S. and over our forces overseas—Taiwan Strait, for example, Persian Gulf, other places—could be an extremely useful approach.

Mr. SAXTON. Thank you, Mr. Chairman.

The CHAIRMAN. Mr. Johnson, from Georgia.

Mr. JOHNSON. Thank you, Mr. Chairman.

Dr. Graham, I would ask you to give us your opinion on what would be the level of knowledge generally of state and local law enforcement agencies about the EMP phenomenon.

Dr. GRAHAM. It varies over a wide range of knowledge, from no familiarity at all to a few states that have taken this very seriously and are making plans of their own. In particular, the State of Maryland and the State of Alaska have worked with their National Guard units, their adjutants general in their states, their legislatures, and their government to begin implementing plans to understand the effects of an EMP attack and to integrate it in the state's emergency planning functions, and we are trying to work with other states, with the adjutants general and others, to expand the state knowledge.

And let me ask General Lawson, who is here, if he has any other comments on the state-related activities.

Mr. JOHNSON. And if you could perhaps speak into the microphone.

General LAWSON. I think we have discussed, in front of the adjutant generals and the other state emergency action officers, in some detail, the kinds of activities that should be included in the emergency actions training programs for state police, for state firemen, for other emergency participants. We have presented, three times, to Homeland Security our thoughts on some of these preparation activities, and, quite candidly, I would hope that they get as much publicity as possible, because that is a part of what many of the commissioners think is a vital portion of our response to this threat, and that being a clear understanding that we, as a Nation, are attempting to develop responses that will minimize the capability itself. We haven't been as successful in getting that prioritized as highly as it should be amongst not only all of the states, but even at the national level.

I think one other action—and it is not a part of the question— but one other action that is appropriate to mention: we have had a continuing dialogue with the utilities and with the Federal Emergency Regulatory Commission on developing a set of procedures that would begin to look at the phase-out of certain portions of the electrical grid—in their timely phase-out—to bring in new equipment at those scheduled phase-outs that are more protected to this emergency.

I think, from your standpoint, the one thing that I would mention that is important for the Armed Services Committee is to understand that all of your bases and all of your military forces, all of them have a great amount of their power that comes through the national grid. All of them have emergency backups, but those backups are very short-lived. And so, what happens to that national grid vitally influences all of our Armed Forces. And that overlap between Homeland Security and the Defense Department needs to be examined very carefully in this particular area, and that is an area where the committee could put a little pressure on both sides of that coin, to improve that emergency capability for the Armed Forces.

Mr. JOHNSON. Thank you. I will yield back.

The CHAIRMAN. Mr. Wilson.

Mr. WILSON. Thank you, Mr. Chairman.

And thank you, Dr. Graham, General Lawson, for your participation in the entire commission. And I greatly appreciate Dr. Roscoe Bartlett bringing this issue to our attention in a very thoughtful way, raising this issue with the American people.

As we have discussed the effect, possibly, on the United States, what would be the effect, or how can we reduce the effect, if there was an EMP attack over the theater of Iraq or Afghanistan?

Dr. GRAHAM. We have worried about that and tried to address it, to some extent. It seems to us the first thing we need to do is review the status of our military forces—not just the strategic forces, but in the theaters you describe. We also get into the general purpose forces. They are a much more diverse set of systems. And we think that rather than try to harden everything in that set of systems, having a few key elements to maintain command, control, communications, and having a plan to replace items which are failed by the EMP and bring in additional forces and additional systems rapidly, would probably make more sense. That is one of the items being addressed in the Defense Department's analysis, and the final go at this, we would defer to them. But we think it is important that the general purpose forces and the theater forces not be ignored in this process.

Mr. WILSON. And as we think of protection for the American people, recovery in the event of an EMP attack—I appreciate Congressman Spratt raised the issue—what can we do on this committee? What can DOD do? I appreciate Congressman Johnson raising the issue of the first responders and the National Guard.

As we look ahead, what can individual families do, in a prudent way, to protect themselves?

Dr. GRAHAM. I have worked on EMP for an embarrassingly long time, Mr. Wilson—over 45 years. About a decade ago, my house in Virginia was hit by lightning, and I lost several pieces of electronics. This is almost as bad as an electrical engineer being electrocuted. It is considered bad form in the profession, and I shouldn't have let that happen.

You can provide local terminal protection for electronics devices. The problem is if there is no electric power, most of those devices aren't going to work anyway. More than that—and myself, I have my own electric generator that I keep disconnected from everything, so it doesn't look like it is attached to antennas. Any conductor would be an antenna. I try to keep enough food and water around to go for several weeks for myself and my family. And those are at least starting steps that can be taken. But to tell you the truth, we have not focused on the individual response to this as much as we have to the government and industry response. But I think it is a good question, and we will go back and reflect on that.

Mr. WILSON. And indeed, I represent coastal areas like Hilton Head Island, where a number of people would have generators. And so, inadvertently, we have significant communities across the United States that have had power interruptions or threats of power interruption due to natural disturbances.

It was brought up about vehicles, cars, and trucks. Will they operate, or are they permanently inoperable?

Dr. GRAHAM. There is some experience with both those things happening. We tested about 50 vehicles. About 10 of them—and we only tested them to 25 kilovolts per meter, which is the kind of threat you would get from more ordinary designs of nuclear weapons—about 10 percent of them stopped running when we tested them at that level. All but one or two of them could be restarted by just switching off the power and then switching on the key again. The computer basically stops the car, but it can be reset by turning off the power. There were one or two of them that actually had computer chip failures in the vehicle and had to be towed back to the dealership to have the chips replaced.

It may not sound too bad, but if you think about what happens to the traffic, say, in the D.C. area on a given morning, when there are 3 or 4 accidents, you can imagine 10 percent of the vehicles on the road suddenly not running anymore. I suspect that would lead to a large number of further accidents and incidents. And so it would be a while before those vehicles would have good transportation access again.

But leaving vehicles turned off, parked, is about the best you can do with cars you already have, and encouraging Detroit to continue to make cars so they are not vulnerable to the transients is another good step.

Mr. WILSON. Thank you very much.

The CHAIRMAN. Mr. Kline.

Mr. KLINE. Thank you, Mr. Chairman.

Thank you, Dr. Graham. And to all of the team, great work. Very distinguished panel.

I want to pick up where Mr. Wilson just left off, and that is with vehicles. I am reading in your report, quote, "Police services will be stretched extremely thin because of a combination of factors. Police will be called on to assist rescue workers removing people from immediate dangers." Failures of automobiles and traffic control systems with the intended massive traffic jams was what you were describing there. If you had a 10 percent failure in Washington, D.C., or 1 percent failure in Washington, D.C., you would have a mess. But it seems also that you can have your ambulances and the fire trucks and the response vehicles themselves would not function. And in your example of the cases where you had the computer chip—which is everywhere now in every modern vehicle—no longer working, you towed it back to the dealer and had a new one put in. But in the scenario we are talking about, I am trying to envision how that would work—that you tow it back to the dealer, and all the chips in the dealership are destroyed.

So, if we had an EMP event of the magnitude that Mr. Bartlett was talking about and you were talking about earlier, significant explosion over Kansas or something like that, isn't it possible that you would have not just stuck elevators, but you would have your ability to respond at all, not just because you couldn't talk, but because you couldn't drive?

Dr. GRAHAM. Yes. I think that is the bottom line, Mr. Kline. On the one hand, the chips that are still in the part bins, if they are not connected to anything else, would probably survive. Wires, circuits, pipes—anything conducting connected to an electrical or electronic device looks like an antenna to an EMP. It conducts the power into the device. That is why I keep the portable generator I have disconnected from everything else at my home.

But there are many things that are connected to wires, et cetera, that have to be—we did test traffic control device—traffic signals, and what we found is those little buttons you push to get the signal to walk across the street are wonderful antennas for EMP and take a destructive level of signal right into the traffic control unit and burn it out.

During the 2003 blackout, the traffic in Manhattan became a gridlock because of traffic signals basically failing from lack of power. There was a telecommunications—it is called a telecommunications hotel, a big telecommunications telephone switching station that had four hours worth of battery power on hand. The phone company had a plan to take a portable generator and connect it to that telephone switching center to keep it going. It had to get that generator halfway across Manhattan, and it was not able to do so in four hours, and the telephone switching system went down. So, that is the kind of problem you are going to see.

Mr. KLINE. It is a pretty tough scenario.

Let me follow up again with Mr. Wilson's thought about the general purpose forces. I know it is used in Afghanistan and Iraq, but they ride around in vehicles with chips, as well. So, presumably, it is not just their command and control, but you could have the vehicles stop. This is the Armed Services Committee. Are there things that we should be pressing? Is there a way to harden that in the vehicle? Or should the Pentagon be making sure there are plenty of chips unconnected, you know, back in the warehouse, so they can be replaced relatively quickly? I can see entire battalions, brigades literally coming to a halt.

Dr. GRAHAM. I think having adequate spares in the area would be very valuable and not hugely expensive, but, also, the vehicles are often designed to be able to withstand a fairly high level of EMP—the military vehicles, the Humvees, the Bradleys, M–1 tanks, and so on. However, normally, they are designed to be protected when they are all closed up or "buttoned up," as the Army says. We have noticed they are generally operated not buttoned up, with things open on them. And so we would encourage the service to do the test. And when they retrofit these vehicles, which they are doing a lot now on the reset programs—refurbishing them, to put enough protection in the vehicles, shielding on the wire harnesses, for example—that they can continue to operate even when they are not buttoned up.

Mr. KLINE. Thank you very much.

Thank you, Mr. Chairman.

The CHAIRMAN. Before I call on Mr. Taylor, let me ask you, Dr. Graham, have you thought about—should the unthinkable happen—communications? What would be left communication-wise? Who could communicate with whom and over what distance and in what manner?

Dr. GRAHAM. We have looked at the commercial telecommunications system, and we think a lot of the calls in progress or being made at the time of the event would stop. Some of the telecommunications equipment would continue, at least as long as its power is available. But we can't predict where the nodes would be still functional and where they wouldn't.

To get around this problem several decades ago, the idea of diverse routing of packet switch networks was invented as a concept. It was actually invented as a Cold War concept, to deal with communications nodes being destroyed by direct attack, in fact. And so, at least, my estimate is that the packet switching network that provides the carrier for the Internet would be the most likely way to sustain some kind of connectivity. But the individual nodes themselves are not, in large part, not designed to be hardened to EMP. So, it would only be a chance that there was a route through the system that would go from you to point B to carry the message.

There is, also, for the military forces, the Milstar satellite system. And perhaps I could ask Dr. Soper, who worked on that and saved it from cancellation at least twice, to talk about that as a continuing military communications capability. Take my seat.

Mr. SOPER. Thank you, Dr. Graham.

I am Gordon Soper. I spent most of my life and career in the Department of Defense. And the question relates to its command and control of our military forces and perhaps, in particular, our nuclear forces.

We have paid a great deal of attention to that. After all, our nuclear weapons are a linchpin of our national security, and it has been uppermost in the Nation's mind to make sure that those weapons are command and controlled through all levels of conflict. And to that end, the Department of Defense has developed a set of standards—in particular the MIL–STD–188, 125 series, the MIL–STD–1269(b)—don't want to get into the details—to direct those people that are responsible for our command and control of nuclear weapons know-how to protect against this threat. And in its basic form, it is really very simple. It tends to be a shielded volume with a minimum number of penetrations, and those penetrations that you can't avoid, you protect. And you test it over and over again. And the most boring part, but, perhaps, the most important, is that you maintain that protection over the life cycle of the system, and that just requires attention to detail, not poking holes in the shield, not disconnecting things.

Fiber optics has been a help in this process. I hope that that has helped address the problem. The Milstar system, the Milstar satellite system, was designed to be hardened or survivable against direct radiation—the X-rays and gamma rays that come out of the weapons and proceed unabated through the vacuum of space. And as Dr. Graham correctly pointed out, one of the more important issues, from an EMP perspective, is not necessarily the satellites, but, rather, the ground systems that collect the information from the satellites and distribute them to the places they need to go.

Hope that addressed your question.

The CHAIRMAN. Thank you so much.

Mr. Taylor.

Mr. TAYLOR. Thank you again, Mr. Chairman, for holding this committee, and I want to thank again my colleague, Mr. Bartlett, for making everyone on this committee aware of a very real threat. I want to thank the panel.

Dr. Graham, a couple of things. I was very much aware that when it came to body armor, up-armored Humvees, improvised explosive device (IED) jammers, and, most recently, Mine Resistant Ambush Protected vehicles, it really wasn't the DOD coming to Congress, saying, "We need these things." It was because of different circumstances Congress telling the DOD, "You are not doing enough." And I don't say that happily, but it is a fact.

In this instance, even though you are going to make a report to the DOD, based on those four scenarios, I don't have a high degree of confidence that, for whatever reasons, they are going to come to us and say, "This is what we need." So, what I would ask of you as a part of your final report is I would hope that a part of your final report is a memo to Congress: "This is what you, members of the Appropriations Committee, members of the Armed Services Committee, need to be doing."

The second thing, I thought you touched on something very appropriate. I happen to have lived down where Katrina hit, saw what life without electricity was like for a few weeks. It wasn't pleasant. I was very much interested in your tip to leave your generator unattached to the home. I would think, for the average citizen who is trying to be prudent and is trying to protect themselves from something like this, which is a very real threat—although a horrible threat, but a very real threat—that you would do this Nation a great service if a similar publication was made available or a checklist of what you can do, as an individual, to try to protect yourself, should something like this happen. I think that would be doing a great service, and then get that into the hands of either the Department of Homeland Security or the Northern Command or someone, at least, for those folks who would choose to do so, at least be made aware of what an individual can do to try to take some steps to protect themselves.

And again, I would welcome your thoughts on this. This is a request that I am making to you. I would hope that the committee would back that up, as far as when it comes to what should this committee be doing, as far as authorizing funds, and what should the appropriators be doing, as far as appropriating funds to address the threat to our Nation.

Dr. GRAHAM. Well, thank you, Mr. Taylor. I think that is an excellent suggestion, and I think we could put out something which could be of use both to individuals, homeowners, but also to state and local authorities and their emergency facilities and so on; and we will look to see what is already available and proceed from there.

As far as what Congress can do going forward, this commission is a creature of the Congress. In fact, we follow the same rules other congressional agencies do, and we owe our existence to you. I am struggling with this, because it pains me a little bit to say it, but as a matter of fact, there is a provision in the current defense authorization bill that this committee has put forward which would extend this commission into the future for some few years. I would say that, in my view, Congress and—through the Congress, the creation of this committee has been the principal forcing function on the Administration to take this issue seriously, and so, the fact that you are proposing to move this forward could have a good effect, in that regard.

We all serve pro bono. I live on the West Coast. I like to say this is fun, but it isn't. Nonetheless, I am sure there are, among the commissioners, other members, people who would be willing to continue to serve if, in the judgment of the Congress, that is a useful function.

Mr. TAYLOR. Thank you very much, sir.

The CHAIRMAN. Thank you very much. It is always nice to be reminded that you are our creature, and the champion, of course, on this issue is Roscoe Bartlett, on whom I now call.

Mr. BARTLETT. Thank you very much. I really want to express my appreciation to the chairman, for calling this hearing, and to the commission. As my colleague Mr. McHugh noted, a lot of commissions have sat before us. None of them, I think, have been as high of quality as this commission. I am really impressed.

I just would like a few quick questions, so that we can get some things on the record. When you were talking about the selective survivability of automobiles, that was at 25 kilovolts per meter. At 100 kilovolts per meter, they are probably all gone.

Dr. GRAHAM. We don't know that for a fact. But the people from whom we got the automobiles wanted them back and in working order, so we didn't go higher than that, because we didn't have the budget to buy that many automobiles, in case they all failed.

I think, in the future, it would be worth Department of Homeland Security carrying out a more thorough set of tests and, perhaps, using some of their own fleet to see what would happen at higher levels. If I had to guess, I would say by the time you got to—certainly to 100 and possibly to 50 kilovolts per meter, you would have quite a few more failures.

Mr. BARTLETT. Thank you.

Our commercial aircraft are not hardened. So the presumption would be all of those that are line of sight would fall out of the sky?

Dr. GRAHAM. They are not specifically hardened to EMP. They are tested against lightning strikes, and, in fact, they experience lightning strikes, as I recall, an average of something like once a year. So, they do have a reasonably good level of EMP protection, as far as flight safety is concerned, and that means, basically, land at the nearest airport after you are hit.

Now, EMP contains some electromagnetic frequencies that are not in lightning strikes, so it is no guarantee that the airplanes will keep working, and as you know, the airplanes are largely software-controlled today—both the engines and the flight controls themselves—so we would probably lose some aircraft. But we would have some that would continue to fly as well.

Mr. BARTLETT. It is my understanding that the usual surge protector does not protect against EMP, because the rise time is in nanoseconds, and it is through the surge protector before it sees it and responds.

Dr. GRAHAM. It depends on the specific surge protector. For example, those designed for lightning only don't have to respond fast enough to protect against EMP. Some others are fast enough to do that.

Mr. BARTLETT. The usual surge protector that protects against lightning probably won't protect you against EMP.

Dr. GRAHAM. Used by whom?

Mr. BARTLETT. The usual surge protector to protect you against lightning probably will not protect you against EMP?

Dr. GRAHAM. It will not necessarily protect you against EMP. When I buy these little surge protection strips for my computers and things of that sort, they claim to work to down to a nanosecond, but I have not seen them tested to that range yet against an EMP-like threat.

Mr. BARTLETT. Satellite vulnerability, because it is so expensive to put weight in orbit—my understanding is that our satellites are usually lower—but satellites are the softest part of this chain—that we probably would lose all of those that were line of sight, close in, from prompt effects, and the others, as you noted, would decay quickly because of pumped-up Van Allen Belts?

Dr. GRAHAM. Yes. Unless the satellite had been specifically designed to be hardened against radiation, including the trapped radiation that would be pumped into the Van Allen Belts, they would all fail within a week or so.

However, many of the ground stations would fail essentially instantaneously, and so we would be out of communication with the satellite even more quickly than the failure of the satellite suggests.

Mr. BARTLETT. Some 90-odd percent of all of our military communications moves over commercial links, satellite links, is my understanding.

Dr. GRAHAM. Let me consult my colleagues here.

Soper, does that sound about right?

Mr. SOPER. Certainly, the military communications that are not critical—I mean, laundry lists and things like that—I don't mean to make light of it—but many noncritical circuits do go over commercial assets.

Dr. GRAHAM. The most critical piece, which we view as strategic command and control, tend to have their own circuits and tend to, in the final analysis, use Milstar as a protected system. But that is—you are getting down to a very small-sized communication channel by the time you get down to that.

Mr. BARTLETT. You mentioned the asymmetric nature of this threat and how we were more vulnerable because we are more sophisticated. If North Korea were to launch a nuclear weapon straight up and detonate it, and that would have an EMP effect on them and on us, without that, our 30-odd thousand people there are probably a match for their million on the other side; is that not correct? We think so.

Dr. GRAHAM. Let us see. I think—several things come to mind. One is that the worst EMP in the northern hemisphere tends to the south of the explosion point, and that is where South Korea is, with respect to North Korea. So, you have picked a particularly damaging scenario for the assets in South Korea. Of course, to meet the North Koreans, we have assets in Korea. The Koreans, South Koreans, have a larger military than we do there. And then, we have assets in Japan, Guam, and other places that we might bring to bear. Of course, the North Koreans know about all those assets.

But it would certainly cause a serious disruption if they launched the attack you described, and they could extend that further if they wished.

Mr. BARTLETT. They are not very sophisticated. They would be much less affected by this attack than our soldiers. They would be relatively all the same size after this attack, or relatively close to it.

Dr. GRAHAM. I don't have detailed information on their communication systems, but certainly, their military systems tend to be much more primitive than ours and, therefore, would be less affected by this.

Mr. BARTLETT. Your generator that is not plugged in would probably not survive a 50 to 100 kilowatt——

Dr. GRAHAM. Fifty to 100 kilovolt per meter.

Probably, it would be okay, as long as I didn't attach any wire to it. It is the need for something that looks, to EMP, like an antenna to get in. That would be the most formidable effect. But somewhere around 100 kilovolts per meter, it has enough wires inside it that it would start being affected.

Mr. BARTLETT. Yeah. In closing, I would just like to reemphasize the discussion that you previously had, relative to individual and family response. I had been concerned that we are paying a little or no attention to the old civil defense. I am a child of the Depression, and I remember the Cold War very well, and I remember everywhere there was a fallout shelter. You couldn't go to any public building without having little brochures there to tell you what to do, and every family knew what they ought to be stockpiling and how they ought to behave in an event like this.

I am very concerned that if we as individuals and families do not know what to do and are not prepared, that every one of us then becomes a ward of the state. And are we not enormously stronger if we are individually and family-wise self-sufficient during an emergency like that?

Dr. GRAHAM. Yes, Mr. Bartlett. I think there are several reasons—several possible threats, both man-made and natural, that could affect us. And having an ability to function in a self-reliant manner for some period of time would benefit us all.

Mr. BARTLETT. Do you think that you could be effective in encouraging our Homeland Security people to become more aggressive in this civil defense role?

Dr. GRAHAM. I met with Senator Lieberman yesterday, as the chairman of the Homeland Security Committee in the other House of Congress, and he was very interested in this subject and agreed to consider it as part of his purview for Homeland Security. So, we will try to continue to work with the Homeland Security functions both in the Congress and the Administration and encourage them to take useful steps.

Mr. BARTLETT. I would just like to note, Mr. Chairman, that if you are preparing for something like this in advance, say, years ahead, you are now a patriot, you are stimulating the economy, but if you do it hours before it happens, now you are a hoarder, and you are doing exactly the same thing; and timing is very critical there now, isn't it?

Thank you very much.

The CHAIRMAN. Mr. Bartlett, thank you.

And, Dr. Graham, thank you, as well as members of your commission.

Oh, excuse me. Mr. Saxton has another question.

Mr. SAXTON. I just wanted to take a minute to thank you for being here and to ask you if—Mr. Taylor mentioned something—actually, Mr. Taylor and I were talking about this earlier this morning. I have an article here, which Mr. Taylor made reference to, and it brings up a subject which I think is extremely interesting and important.

It talks about brain injuries that result from IEDs that Mr. Taylor also mentioned. And this article suggests that brain injuries that have occurred in Iraq seem to be different than brain injuries that have occurred over the years in automobile accidents and other types of happenings.

And EMP is one of the areas that the Defense Advanced Research Projects Agency (DARPA) is currently looking at in terms of its potential effect, with regard to brain injuries. I will just read this one paragraph to you. I found it very interesting.

"Ling's team"—that is the scientist—"will soon begin studying other potential causes of brain injury, such as electromagnetic pulses. If EMP from a blast is powerful enough, it can interfere with nearby electronic devices. 'The brain is an electronic organ,' says Ling. 'If an EMP pulse can take out a radio, why not short-circuit a brain?'"

So, I guess what I would like to just ask or suggest is that, maybe, inasmuch as our authorization bill extends your commission, maybe it would be a good idea for DARPA and your commission to work together on this, as much as you have got all this experience with studying this subject. And I am sure you would be of great benefit to Dr. Ling and his team. I just mention this to you, and I will certainly see you get a copy of this article as a starting point.

Dr. GRAHAM. Thank you.

While it is not in our mandate today, it sounds very interesting. I would note that I also serve on a National Academy Board called a Board on Army Science and Technology, which—and the National Academy has the resources of the National Institute of Medicine as well as the National Academy of Sciences, the National Academy of Engineering, so it can bring a very diverse set of talents together. And this sounds like the kind of question that might be directed to the National Academies and to the Board on Army Science and Technology, to work with the scientists and the government.

Mr. SAXTON. Thank you.

The CHAIRMAN. Again, Dr. Graham, thank you and your commission for your excellent work, not just today, for appearing, but for the work that you have done through the months on the commission. And we are most appreciative, and we will be in touch with you and the commission again.

If there are no further questions, the meeting is adjourned. Thank you.

Dr. GRAHAM. Thank you, Mr. Chairman.

[Whereupon, at 11:58 p.m., the committee was adjourned.]

APPENDIX

JULY 10, 2008

PREPARED STATEMENTS SUBMITTED FOR THE RECORD

JULY 10, 2008

TESTIMONY OF
DR. WILLIAM R. GRAHAM

TO THE
HOUSE ARMED SERVICES COMMITTEE

THURSDAY, JULY 10, 2008
10:00 AM

DR. WILLIAM R. GRAHAM
CHAIRMAN
COMMISSION TO ASSESS THE THREAT
TO THE
UNITED STATES
FROM
ELECTROMAGNETIC PULSE (EMP) ATTACK
STATEMENT BEFORE THE
HOUSE ARMED SERVICES COMMITTEE
July 10, 2008

Mr. Chairman, Members of the Committee, thank you for the opportunity to testify today on behalf of the Commission to Assess the Threat to the United States from Electromagnetic Pulse (EMP) Attack, established through the initiative of the House Armed Services Committee, mandated by the Congress in the Floyd D. Spence National Defense Authorization Act for Fiscal Year 2001 (Public Law 106-398), and subsequently reestablished in the National Defense Authorization Act for Fiscal Year 2006 (Public Law 109-163).

BACKGROUND

In accord with our statutory mandate, the Commission is composed of nine members, seven of whom were appointed by the Secretary of Defense and two of whom were appointed by the Director of the Federal Emergency Management Agency. In selecting individuals for appointment to the Commission, the Secretary of Defense was also directed to "consult with the chairmen and ranking minority members of the Committees on Armed Services of the Senate and House of Representatives."

An executive report produced by the EMP Commission and delivered to Congress in 2004 provided an overview of the EMP threat to the U.S., its friends and allies, and its deployed forces. Part of the purpose of my testimony today is to introduce a new report produced by the EMP Commission. This report presents the results of the Commission's assessment of an EMP attack on our critical national infrastructures, and provides recommendations for preparation, monitoring, protection, and recovery from such an attack. The assessment is informed by analytic and test activities executed under Commission sponsorship, which are discussed in the report. Four other EMP Commission reports were delivered to Congress in 2004, all classified, describing the status of the EMP threat over the next fifteen years as directed by our statutory mandate, and discussing the posture of U.S. military forces with respect to EMP.

Recent disturbing events involving the command and control of nuclear weapons have demonstrated the problems that can occur when the nation does not pay adequate attention to nuclear weapon matters. These problems reflect a shift in culture and attitudes regarding nuclear weapons and their role in today's world. Our increased vulnerability to EMP is also a result of U.S. reliance on increasingly sophisticated commercial technologies that have not been designed to withstand the stresses generated by an electromagnetic pulse attack. The Commission has identified important vulnerabilities in our nation's critical infrastructures, which are essential to both our civilian and military capabilities.

SUMMARY

It is the consensus of the EMP Commission that the Nation need not be vulnerable to catastrophic consequences of an EMP attack. As detailed in the Commission report provided today to the Congress, the Nation's vulnerability to EMP that gives rise to potentially large-scale, long-term consequences can be reasonably reduced below the level of a potentially catastrophic national problem by coordinated and focused effort between the private and public sectors of our country. The cost for such improved security in the next 3 to 5 years is modest by any standard—and extremely so in relation to both the war on terror and the value of the national infrastructures threatened.

The appropriate response to the EMP threat is a balance of prevention, planning, training, maintaining situational awareness, protection, and preparations for recovery. Such actions are both feasible and well within the Nation's means and resources to accomplish, and would provide further benefits to the U.S. by increasing the reliability of our critical national infrastructures and preparing them to manage the effects of other large-scale, widespread threats, both man-made, such as cyber attack, and naturally caused, such as very large-scale hurricanes and geomagnetic storms. However, if the EMP threat is unaddressed, the current status of U.S. critical national infrastructures can both invite and reward attack.

DISCUSSION

Although EMP was first considered during the "Cold War" as a means of paralyzing U.S. retaliatory forces, the risk of an EMP attack may be greater today than during the Cold War, as several adversaries seek nuclear weapons, ballistic missiles, and asymmetric ways to overcome U.S. conventional superiority using one or a small number of nuclear weapons.

The electromagnetic fields produced by weapons deployed with the intent to produce EMP have a high likelihood of damaging electrical power systems, electronics, and information systems upon which American society depends. Their effects on critical infrastructures could be sufficient to qualify as catastrophic to the Nation.

It is my hope that the Commission's work can help play a role in restoring a national consensus on the need to take nuclear threats seriously – including the threat posed by an EMP attack – and to strengthen U.S. efforts to deal with that threat. In so doing, the U. S. will reduce the incentives for adversaries to contemplate conducting such an attack on our homeland, our friends and allies, and our forces deployed abroad.

A high-altitude electromagnetic pulse results from the detonation of a nuclear warhead at altitudes in the range of about 40 to 400 kilometers above the Earth's surface. The immediate effects of EMP are disruption of, and damage to, electronic systems and electrical infrastructure. EMP is not reported in the scientific literature to have direct physiological effects on people.

EMP and its effects were observed during the U.S. and Soviet exo-atmospheric nuclear test programs in the early 1960s. During the U.S. STARFISH nuclear test at an altitude of about 400 kilometers above Johnston Island,, some electrical systems in the Hawaiian Islands, 1400 kilometers distant, were affected, causing the failure of street lighting systems, tripping of circuit breakers, triggering burglar alarms, and permanent damage to a commercial telecommunications relay facility that caused it to cease functioning.

In their exo-atmospheric nuclear testing, the Soviets executed a series of nuclear detonations in which they exploded 300-kiloton weapons at approximately 300, 150, and 60 kilometers above their test site in South Central Asia. In the 1990s, Russian scientists reported that on each shot they observed damage to overhead and underground buried cables out to distances of 600 kilometers. They also observed surge arrestor burnout, spark-gap breakdown, blown fuses, and power supply breakdowns.

What is significant about an EMP attack is that one or a few high-altitude nuclear detonations can produce EMP effects that can potentially disrupt or damage electronic systems over much of the United States, virtually simultaneously, at a time determined by an adversary. EMP is one of a small number of threats that can hold our society at risk of catastrophic consequences. EMP will cover the wide geographic area within line of sight to the nuclear weapon. It has the capability to produce significant damage to critical infrastructures that support the fabric of U.S. society and the ability of the United States and Western nations to project influence and military power.

The common element that can produce such an impact from EMP is primarily electronics, so pervasive in all aspects of our society and military, coupled through critical infrastructures. Our vulnerability is increasing daily as our use of and dependence on electronics continues to grow in both our civil and military sectors. The impact of EMP is asymmetric in relation to potential antagonists who are not as dependent on advanced electronic technologies.

The current vulnerability of our critical infrastructures can both invite and reward attack if not corrected. Correction is feasible and well within the Nation's means and resources to accomplish.

Several potential adversaries have the capability to attack the United States with a high-altitude nuclear weapon-generated electromagnetic pulse, and others appear to be pursuing efforts to obtain that capability. A determined adversary can achieve an EMP attack capability without having a high level of sophistication. For example, an adversary would not have to have long-range ballistic missiles to conduct an EMP attack against the United States. Such an attack could be launched from a freighter off the U.S. coast using a short- or medium-range missile to loft a nuclear warhead to high-altitude. Terrorists sponsored by a rogue state could attempt to execute such an attack without revealing the identity of the perpetrators. Iran, the world's leading sponsor of international terrorism, has practiced launching a mobile ballistic missile from a vessel in the Caspian Sea. Iran has also tested high-altitude explosions of the Shahab-III, a test mode consistent with EMP attack, and described the tests as successful. Iranian military writings explicitly discuss a nuclear EMP attack that would gravely harm the United States. While the Commission does not know the intention of Iran in conducting these activities, we are disturbed by the capability that emerges when we connect the dots.

Certain types of relatively low-yield nuclear weapons can be employed to generate potentially catastrophic EMP effects over wide geographic areas, and designs for variants of such weapons may have been illicitly trafficked for a quarter-century. Recently, as reported in the press, United Nations investigators found that the design for an advanced nuclear weapon, miniaturized to fit on ballistic missiles currently in the inventory of Iran, North Korea, and other potentially hostile states, was in the possession of Swiss criminals affiliated with the A.Q. Khan nuclear smuggling network.

This fact suggests that other advanced nuclear weapon designs may already be in the possession of hostile states and of states that sponsor terrorism. This fact also suggests that it would be a mistake to judge the status and sophistication of rogue nuclear weapon programs based solely on their indigenous national capabilities, since outside assistance may well have been provided.

Depending on the specific characteristics of the EMP attacks, unprecedented cascading failures of major infrastructures could result. In that event, a regional or national recovery would be long and difficult, and would seriously degrade the safety and overall viability of our Nation. The primary avenues for catastrophic damage to the Nation are through our electric power infrastructure and thence into our telecommunications, energy, transportation, and other infrastructures. These, in turn, can seriously impact other important aspects of our Nation's life, including the financial system; means of getting food, water, and medical care to the citizenry; trade and production of goods and services. The recovery of any one of the key national infrastructures is dependent upon the recovery of others. The longer the outage, the more problematic and uncertain the recovery will be. It is possible for the functional outages to become mutually reinforcing until at some point the degradation of infrastructure could have irreversible effects on the country's ability to support its population.

Given our armed forces' reliance on critical national infrastructures (e.g., electric power, telecommunications, food and water, etc.), a cascading failure of these infrastructures could seriously jeopardize our military's ability to execute its missions in support of our national security Projection of military power from air bases and seaports requires electricity, fuel, food and water, and the coordination of military operations depends upon telecommunications and information systems, that are also indispensable to society as a whole. Within the U.S., these assets are in most cases obtained by the military from our critical national infrastructures.

EMP effects from nuclear bursts are not new threats to our nation. What is different now is that some potential sources of EMP threats are difficult to deter—they can be terrorist groups that have no state identity, have only one or a few weapons, and are motivated to attack the U.S. without regard for their own safety. Potentially hostile states, such as North Korea and Iran, may also be developing the capability to pose an EMP threat to the United States, and may also be unpredictable and difficult to deter.

China and Russia have considered limited nuclear attack options that, unlike their Cold War plans, employ EMP as the primary or sole means of attack. Indeed, in May 1999, during the NATO bombing of former Yugoslavia, high-ranking members of the Russian Duma, meeting with a U.S. congressional delegation to discuss the Balkans conflict, raised the specter of a Russian EMP attack that would paralyze the United States. As recently as two weeks ago, Assistant Secretary of Defense for Asian and Pacific Security Affairs James J. Shinn testified before this Committee that China's arms buildup is increasing the danger of a future conflict over Taiwan. Mr. Shinn disclosed that China's military is working on exotic electromagnetic pulse (EMP) weapons that can devastate electronic systems using a burst of energy similar to that produced by a nuclear blast. "The consequence of EMP is that you destroy the communications network," Mr. Shin said. "And we are, as you know, and as the Chinese also know, heavily dependent on sophisticated communications, satellite communications, in the conduct of our forces. And so, whether it's from an EMP or it's some kind of a coordinated [anti-satellite] effort, we could be in a very bad place if the Chinese enhanced their capability in this area," he concluded.

U.S. military forces, allies, or interests could also be affected inadvertently by an EMP attack between other actors in a conflict not involving the United States, as in hostilities between India and Pakistan, for example.

Another key difference from the past is that the U.S. has developed more than most other nations as a modern society heavily dependent on electric power, electronics, telecommunications, information networks, and an extensive set of financial and transportation systems that leverage modern technology. This asymmetry is a source of substantial economic, industrial, and societal advantages for the U.S. But the critical interdependencies and normally reliable operation of the infrastructures create potential vulnerabilities if multiple, simultaneous disruptions and failures can be made to occur.

Therefore, terrorists or state actors that possess one or a few relatively unsophisticated nuclear armed missiles may well calculate that, instead of or in addition to destroying a city or military base, they could obtain the greatest economic-political-military utility from conducting an EMP attack.

The time required for full recovery of service would depend on both the damage to the electric power infrastructure and to other critical national infrastructures. Larger affected areas and stronger EMP field strengths will prolong the time to recover. Some critical electric power components are no longer manufactured in the United States, and their acquisition ordinarily requires up to a year of lead-time in routine circumstances. Damage to or loss of these components could leave significant parts of the electric power grid out of service for months to a year or more. There is a point at which the shortage or exhaustion of sustaining backup systems, including emergency power supplies, standby fuel supplies, communications, and manpower resources, leads to a continuing degradation of critical infrastructures for a prolonged period, with highly adverse consequences to our population and forces.

The ability to recover from an EMP attack is complicated by increasing sophistication and automation that has made manpower less necessary to running the critical national infrastructures. The use of automated control systems has allowed many companies and utilities to operate effectively with small work forces. Thus, while manual control of some systems may be possible, the number of people knowledgeable enough to support manual operations is limited. Repair of physical damage is also constrained by a small work force. Many maintenance crews are sized to perform routine and preventive maintenance of high-reliability equipment that is not expected to fail simultaneously over a widespread area. When repair or replacement is required that exceeds routine levels, arrangements are typically in place to augment crews from outside the affected area. However, due to the simultaneous, geographically widespread effects from EMP, many workers will be occupied in their own areas, and unavailable to help other areas. Thus, repairs normally requiring weeks of effort may require a much longer time.

In closing, allow me to give a preview of the EMP Commission's findings to date for its next report, due to Congress in November, which will assess the progress being made to protect the Nation from EMP attack.

The Commission requested and received information from a number of Federal agencies and Department of Energy National Laboratories. We received information from the North American Electric Reliability Corporation, the President's National Security Telecommunications Advisory Committee, the National Communications System, the Federal Reserve Board, the Department of Defense, the Department of Homeland Security, and the Intelligence Community. While it benefited from these inputs, the Commission developed an independent assessment, and is solely responsible for the content of its research, conclusions, and recommendations.

Early in this review it became apparent that only limited EMP vulnerability testing had been accomplished for modern electronic systems and components. To partially remedy this deficit, the Commission sponsored illustrative testing of current systems and infrastructure components. The Commission's view is that the Federal Government does not today have sufficient human and physical assets for reliably assessing and managing EMP threats.

While measures to establish a balance of prevention, planning, training, maintaining situational awareness, protection, and preparations for recovery from an EMP attack will require a sustained effort, the Commission wishes to note an increased focus within the Department of Defense since it received our earlier reports. Our report to the Congress, due in November, will address this in more detail as part of the Commission's required assessment of DoD's progress in implementing steps to mitigate the risk of EMP attack. In particular, the Commission takes note of revived DoD efforts to address survivability concerns of weapons systems considering chemical, biological, radiological, and nuclear effects.

CONCLUSION

The United States faces a long-term challenge to maintain technical competence for understanding and managing the effects of nuclear weapons, including EMP. The Department of Energy and the National Nuclear Security Administration have developed and implemented an extensive Nuclear Weapons Stockpile Stewardship Program over the last decade. However, no comparable effort was initiated to understand the effects that nuclear weapons produce on modern systems. The Commission reviewed current national capabilities to understand and to manage the effects of EMP and concluded that the U.S. is rapidly losing the technical competence and facilities that it needs in the Government, the National Laboratories, and the Industrial Community.

An EMP attack on the critical national infrastructures is a serious problem, but one that can be managed in an orderly way at reasonable cost. A serious national commitment to address the threat of an EMP attack can lead to a national posture that would significantly reduce the payoff for such an attack and allow the United States to recover from EMP, and from other threats, man-made and natural, to the critical national infrastructures. A failure to do so will not only leave the critical infrastructures necessary for our society to function at risk but will also place our ability reliably to conduct military operations in jeopardy.

This concludes my prepared statement. Thank you again, Mr. Chairman, for the opportunity to present the Commission views and for your support of our efforts.

At this time, I would be happy to respond to any questions you have.